# The Journey

# The Journey

Cathy Gwynn

THE JOURNEY
by Cathy Gwynn
Published by Creation House Press
A Part of Strang Communications Company
600 Rinehart Road
Lake Mary, FL 32746
www.creationhouse.com





Author photograph by Soreyrith Um
Cover design by Terry Clifton
Book design by David Bilby

Library of Congress Control Number: 2002108644

International Standard Book Number: 0884199363

Printed in the United States of America

02 03 04 05 5 4 3 2 1

*For God so loved the world that He gave His only begotten Son, that whoever believes in Him should not perish but have everlasting life.*

—JOHN 3:16

# Contents

# The Journey

There are defining moments in some people's lives when everything that has been—and everything that will be—comes down to a single point in time when they choose their course. My moment came on May 23, 2001.

I was driving home from a meeting at PUSH, an advertising agency I consult with, when the call from Lydia came in on my cell phone. I remember looking at the clock and seeing that it was 4:20 P.M.

"Cathy, have you heard from Dennis?" she asked, trying to hold back the alarm in her voice. She and Dennis both worked for his brother David's company, so at first I thought the call was business related.

"No, not since last night when he called to tell me he'd made it into Tallahassee and gave me the number of the hotel where he was staying," I replied.

"Cathy, we can't find him. I didn't want to call you until we'd tried everything. But he didn't show up for his meetings and he's not at the hotel. I've called the police...and the hospitals...and we can't find him."

I heard the words, but they didn't make sense. It was as if I were hearing something about someone else. This just wasn't like Dennis.

Dennis had called me at around 6:25 P.M. the night before and told me he was going to have dinner at the house of a coworker named John. Almost in a daze, I remembered that he had told me that John had just gotten a great job with Microsoft. After Dennis gave me the number to the hotel, he had said, "Call me later if you want" ...*just as he always did when we were apart.*

But our 21-month-old son, Chase, had kept me up late...so I never called him back.

As I drove through my neighborhood, I tried to make sense of Lydia's call. *How could anything be wrong? Wouldn't I know it? Wouldn't I feel something?*

By the time I pulled into our driveway, I was praying desperately, "God, please let Dennis be OK, let him be OK."

I called Dennis's cell phone the moment I stopped the car, but there was no answer—just the comforting, familiar sound of his voice on his voicemail message, the one I had heard so many times before.

Now frantic, I left him a message. "Den, *please* call me. We can't find you. Where are you? *Please* call me."

As the fear sank in, I started turning numb. Dad was in the house watching Chase. I told him that Dennis was missing—the words sounding strange coming out of my mouth...as if someone else were speaking. Thankfully,

Chase was taking a nap, so I didn't have to worry about hiding my fear from him as I tried desperately to grasp what was happening.

Dad held me in his arms and my mind raced. Nothing made sense. *Could this be real? Is this really happening?* I felt like reality was slowly disengaging.

Needing to do something, I went into my office and called American Express and our bank to see if Dennis had used his credit cards. As my fear escalated into panic, I imagined someone had carjacked him and was doing terrible things to him. *He might be afraid right now, or hurt...*

My thoughts were interrupted when Lydia called back. They had tracked down John. Dennis had left his house some time after 11:00 P.M. *That was just a few hours after I talked to him on the phone.*

I felt some sense of relief after both American Express and First Union said his cards had not been used in the last couple of days.

*But what did that mean? Where was he?* Nothing made sense.

I was having trouble thinking straight as I dialed Lydia's number to tell her what I'd learned about the charge cards.

Just as she answered the phone, I looked out the window and saw a police car driving slowly past my house. After a minute or so, I looked out the window again. That's when I saw the uniformed officer and a plainclothes officer walking across our driveway. Because they were approaching from my neighbors' house and my neighbors were with them, my first thought was that something was wrong in the neighborhood...but in my heart I think I knew.

I made my way to the front door. Chase was up and Dad was holding him. I still had the phone in my hand and Lydia was asking me what was going on and why the police were there.

As I opened the door, everything started to spin.

The officer's face was so solemn. I couldn't process what he was saying as he walked in and motioned for me to sit down on the couch.

Lydia kept asking me what was going on.

"I don't know, but they want me to sit down," was all I could manage to say.

My mind was scrambling to make sense of it all, but I couldn't. It was like reality had suddenly vanished. My neighbors, John and Judy, sat down next to me, one on each side. The officer started talking in a low and matter-of-fact voice, but Chase was crying and Lydia was panicking in my ear. I couldn't hear what he was saying.

The officer started over...I could tell that it was hard for him.

The only words I remember were "fatal accident" and "died instantly."

"No!" I screamed.

My neighbors were crying, hugging me. I could still hear Lydia's voice. She was almost screaming.

"What? What happened to Dennis?" she demanded.

"He's dead," I sobbed.

Unable to comprehend what I had said, she asked me

to repeat it; but I couldn't bear to say those awful, horrifying words again. All I could do was hand the phone to the officer and say, "Would you please tell his mother?"

Chase was hysterical, but he was my saving grace because I had to pull myself together for him. I tried having Dad take him into the other room—but Chase needed me. I held my son and comforted him, but I was completely numb.

I remember only some of what happened next. I remember the policeman saying he had some information that we would probably want to write down. I got him some paper and a pen. His fellow officer asked Dad and me if they could call anyone for us...maybe our pastor.

Dad said he would call the pastor.

I couldn't think. I was holding Chase and explaining to him that the policemen were there to help us. He had stopped crying, but he knew something was very wrong. The policemen were nice and very compassionate, but they were powerless to do anything. Having them in my house began to make me feel nauseated. I didn't want to know any details; I just wanted to get away from them and from everything. But I couldn't do that because I had to take care of my son.

I think my friend Danica was the first person I told. I called her and asked if Chase could come to her house and play for a while with her daughter. Then I had to tell her why.

I had to force the words out of my mouth: "Dennis was killed in a car accident in Tallahassee," I heard myself saying.

I was so grateful when she came and got Chase. Once he was gone, I went into my bathroom and stood in front of the mirror with tears streaming down my face.

I sobbed, "Please don't leave me. *Please! Don't leave me.* I can't do this by myself. It's not supposed to be like this. Please don't leave me."

Inside, I was screaming; but I didn't want to scream out loud.

Questions raced through my head: *How can I go on without him? How can I be a single mom? How will Chase grow up without his dad? How can this possibly be happening to us? How can I be a widow at 35?*

I walked into the bedroom and called his cell phone again—just to hear his voice.

*How can he be gone? How can I never hear his voice again? What if I forget what it sounded like? How can I never touch him again?*

I sank down on the floor next to the bed and sobbed. Finally I got up and walked to our bedroom window. The blinds were closed, but some of the early evening light was streaming through.

As I stood there, I praised God. I glorified Him and I thanked Him for His mercy. I remembered the scripture that's written on a picture that hangs in my home office, "Cast thy burden upon the Lord and He shall sustain thee; he shall never suffer the righteous to be moved" (Psalm 55:22, KJV).

After I recited the scripture to myself, I prayed, "Lord, I am casting it all on You. I give it all to You—all of my grief, my fear, everything. And I am trusting You to sustain me."

That was my defining moment. I had a choice. I could try to handle this on my own—and risk falling victim to anger and depression and despair—or I could give it all to the Lord, trusting that He would get me through it, that His promise of salvation is real.

In that instant, when I let go of everything and surrendered it to God, I felt a peace. I knew that this was part of God's plan. That realization didn't take away the pain and sorrow, but it helped me know there was a purpose in it.

And I knew I could go on.

## THE GIFT OF DIVINE REVELATION

Each of us has spiritual gifts. For a long time I wondered what mine were. Over the years, however, I have discovered that I am blessed with the gift of knowledge, or revelation. (See 1 Corinthians 12:8.) In fact, somehow I've always known that I would lose my husband. Whenever knowledge of that would come into my head, I would always suppress it, because I didn't want to believe it and felt guilty for having such horrible thoughts. But, that's just one of things that I have "known."

Let me try to explain. When God blesses me with bits of knowledge, it's like there is just one piece of information I *know*—throughout my whole being—to be true. It is so clear to me that it's as if I've always known it to be true, even though it has just been revealed to me.

But knowledge about losing my husband was, in

actuality, a confirmation that this had always been a part of God's plan. And knowing that his death actually confirmed what I had always known to be true was, in some ways, reassuring. You may be wondering how I could possibly say that. But I am hoping my story will help explain how having a glimpse of the sovereign and divine plan of God can indeed be reassuring, especially during our darkest moments.

Some people may think that God was cruel for taking Dennis when He did, but I hope you will discover that my story is really a testament to how loving God is. I hope you will find that my experience freed something that had been locked inside me.

After surrendering my grief and fear to God, I left the window and walked back toward my bathroom.

"God, please let me know that he is in heaven," I prayed repeatedly.

And God was quick to answer me, saying, "You already know the answer to that."

(Let me try to explain what it's like when God speaks to you through His Holy Spirit. It's not like hearing a big, booming voice. Instead, you hear your own voice in your head, but the thoughts are not yours. You sense that the words are from God. If you are a young Christian, as I was when I first started hearing His voice, you may wonder whether the words you hear are yours or God's. I've found that, when the words are God's, He always confirms the message in some way.)

Even though God had told me that I already knew the answer to my own question, I asked Him to let me know, beyond a shadow of a doubt, that Dennis was in heaven.

And God did just that. In fact, at Dennis's memorial service, I told everyone how God had confirmed this for me three times. Since then, He has actually continued to confirm it to me in various other ways.

## MY FIRST HEAVENLY CONFIRMATION

I knew my first confirmation would come from my mother, because she walks very closely with the Lord. When all of this happened, Mom was in Tacoma, Washington, where she was helping to set up the choir for a Benny Hinn crusade. Knowing that we would need her prayers, Dad had tried to reach her as soon as we found out Dennis was missing; but by the time she was able to return his call, we already knew what had happened.

After taking the red-eye flight home, she walked through my kitchen door and embraced me. Tearfully, she told me how sorry she was.

Then, she said, "But I have something wonderful to share with you."

I knew right then that this was the confirmation I had prayed for.

She told me that when she was at the airport waiting for her flight, she was looking out the window and asking God to let her know that Dennis was in heaven.

As she watched the planes taking off and landing, she resolved to help Chase remember how he and his daddy used to watch the planes together. Then, as she watched a plane in the sky, she said it was as if God took a windshield wiper and wiped clear a view into heaven. She saw Dennis standing there in the presence of God. In awe of what he was seeing and experiencing in God's presence, he exclaimed, "Mrs. Waine, you were right!" It was as if he was saying to her, "You told me so." He was amazed and excited and overjoyed, she said.

You see, when I first started dating Dennis, he had come over to my parents' house for dinner one night and had gotten into a discussion with my mother, saying that he believed in evolution instead of creation. I don't think he actually believed what he was saying; I think he was really more intent on stirring up a good debate. But even if he did believe in evolution then, his view eventually changed.

Dennis would often challenge my mom on spiritual things, and she would take those opportunities to teach him. It all started with that conversation about evolution and culminated with his response to heaven.

Her experience served to confirm what I already knew to be true. And knowing that Dennis is in heaven gives me tremendous peace, because I know that I will see him again. Knowing this also enables me to stand strong against the darkness that tries to creep in.

## Dark Thoughts Attack

That first night as I lay in bed holding Chase, the dark thoughts almost crumbled me. I was haunted by images of Dennis being in the car and hitting the tree. Then I would think of him, all alone in that cold, awful morgue. Each time one of these thoughts entered my head, it felt as if knives were going through my stomach; as though I couldn't breathe.

These are the kinds of thoughts the devil uses to try to break us and then plunge us into despair; to overpower us with the agony of feeling lost. But the Holy Spirit reminded me that those things I was thinking of did not actually happen to Dennis—not to the part of him that makes him "Dennis." Instead, these events only happened to his body. This is a hard concept for some people to grasp, because the body is what we interact with; it is how we visually identify someone. But in reality, what is inside of people, their spirits and their souls, is what makes up who they are. Their spirits and souls, not their bodies, is what causes us to love them, be annoyed by them, laugh with them, think of them as a friend or respect them.

Recently, I was thinking about how I would explain all of this to Chase when he gets a little older. I thought about people who are in accidents and lose the use of their legs. Although those parts of their bodies don't work anymore, what happened to them is only physical—and the physical change doesn't change who they are. Likewise, when a person dies, his body perishes, but *he* does not. So, what happens to his soul and spirit? Eternal destruction is what each of us deserves, but eternal life in heaven is what Jesus offers us. Although it may not make sense to the unbeliever or to those who have not yet walked through what I have recently gone through, my sure knowledge of eternal life through Jesus Christ gave me great peace then. It continues to do so now.

*That your faith should not be in the wisdom of men, but in the power of God.*
—1 Corinthians 2:5

## Faith Makes the Difference

That first night, and in the days that followed—actually, even now—I witnessed what a difference faith makes. I learned firsthand how important it is to present tragic news to people in simple terms that are easy for them to comprehend.

It took great faith for me to do this as I called our friends to tell them what had happened. Each time I dialed a number, I thought, *How do I say this?* I also wondered why we immediately call people to tell them.

I soon realized that I was calling friends because I wanted the people who cared about us to be there for me. And believe me, having others beside me was God's provision during this difficult time.

Each time I called someone I had to say, "Dennis was in a car accident in Tallahassee and was killed."

I felt disembodied—as if I were in a fog—each time I repeated those words. The statement seemed very incomplete, because I knew I wasn't recounting the whole story. But somehow I knew that this was all that people could handle initially.

At first, each person would respond with disbelief. They would say, "What?" and I would have to repeat the news.

My friend Ann kept saying, "What? What?"

I finally said, "Ann, don't make me say it again."

I wasn't able to call all of Dennis's friends, because I didn't have their phone numbers and many weren't listed in the phone book—Dennis knew their numbers by heart. Although I felt a little frustrated about not knowing how to reach them, in some ways I was relieved that I couldn't. On the one hand I wanted them to hear the news from me, but on the other hand, I didn't think I could keep repeating those words.

Chris was the first of Dennis's friends that I had to tell. I also told Dennis's best friend, Toby. Thankfully, Toby and his family were in town visiting his parents, and his parents' number was in the phone book. I had to leave a message for Toby to call me. When he called me back, telling him what had happened turned out to be one of the hardest things for me to do.

Toby had been like a brother to Dennis, and the two of them had many plans and dreams of what they were going to do together. I just praised God that Toby was in town and not at home in South Carolina, because I didn't have his phone number there. I believe that Toby's being in town was also a part of God's plan.

## TRYING TO COMPREHEND WHAT HAD HAPPENED

Although it was only a couple of hours, the gap between when the police came to my house and when family and friends began arriving seemed like ages; as if time were standing still. But I couldn't stay still. After making the necessary phone calls, I wandered aimlessly from one room to another, sobbing and feeling like I was going to collapse.

At some point I went into the backyard and walked in circles, talking to Dennis. It felt good to be outside under the big open sky. For a while I sat in the sandbox Dennis and I had built for Chase. I just sat there, trying to comprehend what was happening to me.

When Dennis's family came over that night, none of us really knew what to do. My jaw hurt from straining and tensing it when I cried and from holding back my screams. We talked about Dennis and remembered the good things about him. We reminisced about some of the things he had done.

Our pastor, Henry Cribb, came by and asked if I needed anything. Angie, Maureen and Laura, from my small group at church, brought food. I think some of the neighbors brought over food that night too; it's all a blur.

One of the things I do remember is Dennis's friend Chris standing in my kitchen with tears in his eyes. The look on his face is forever etched in my memory because it reflected the pain of losing someone dear to you—a true friend. At the time, everyone else in the house was a family member, and we were all in shock. But Chris's eyes said so much to me. I think it was then that the Holy Spirit spoke to me about helping others to know the truth and to understand God's incredible grace, so that they could have peace through Him. Telling you my story is one way of doing just that.

So now, as I share my heart with you, you will see that my story is a testament to 1 John 1:5:

> *This is the message which we have heard from Him and declare to you, that God is light and in Him there is no darkness at all.*

I am hoping that my testimony will help you see His light—even when it seems like you are in the center of the darkest of storms. My desire is for you to abound in the blessing of peace and assurance that God has given me.

# Our Journey of Faith

Faith is a journey that is unique for each of us. To me, faith has always been very personal. I have always believed in God, but I can't remember exactly when I was "saved."

Dennis and I were what I would call "average" Christians. Like me, Dennis used to say that his relationship with God was personal and private. When I pointed out that I was worried about some of the music he was listening to, or how he was skipping church because he had to work, he would tell me, "Cathy, I don't have to go to church every Sunday to have a relationship with God. I have a relationship with Him and I pray." And the truth was, I indeed could see the Holy Spirit subtly moving in his life, especially after Chase was born.

I guess the point that I am trying to make here is that there was nothing special about Dennis and me—we didn't have a deep faith walk. But we had faith. Faith in God, and faith in the salvation that Jesus offers every one who accepts Him.

## Focus on What is Eternal

I can see now—more than ever—the difference that faith makes. It's as if I have been firmly planted in stone and have been forever sealed. But I see others struggling or shutting down completely, and I want to reach out and help them—to help them know and be reassured by the love and mercy of God.

God will use our circumstances to build a relationship with us. If we turn to Him, He will help us to know the love and mercy of Jesus—even in the midst of our pain, our struggles and our doubts. I see friends and family searching, wanting to have stronger faith, desiring to be closer to God. I know that God will use what they are going through, even losing Dennis, to bring them closer to Himself.

Those who don't know the Lord are having the hardest time dealing with the loss. They focus on the accident and the details of Dennis's death, and on everything that is worldly—because those are the only things to which they can relate. They are left tormented and in utter pain.

Because I am focused on what is eternal, I don't want to know, or need to know, the details of the accident; they don't matter to me. The only thing that matters is that Dennis is in heaven and that I will see him again one day. I realize that a lot of people will probably think that I am just a grieving widow, saying these things to comfort herself; that I'm in some sort of denial. But that assessment couldn't be farther from the truth. In fact, I see more clearly now than ever. Knowing that Dennis is in heaven is a tremendous comfort. It doesn't take the pain away, but it does erase the blackness and the torment.

I think the people who have surprised me most are the ones who say they are Christians, but who have a hard time believing some of what I have to share. They study the Bible, go to church, pray—apparently believe in God and in salvation—but to them, faith in God seems to be more theory than reality. When they hear of God's miraculous love, or of Him reaching out to someone they actually know, it's hard for them to believe or accept it.

I just want to shake them and say, "God is real! Get out of that comfort zone and *experience* Him! Hear the glorious things that I have to share and feel His presence and His grace. This is not just for someday, it's for *now*!"

I have a strong feeling—a sense of urgency—that God wants us to really get to know Him. Don't wait. Let Him into your heart. Receive His miracles and blessings now!

## Faith Doesn't Take Away All the Pain

I am not saying that experiencing the reality of God's presence in our daily lives and in the midst of loss will take away your pain. I feel Dennis's loss every day, almost every moment. I feel like half of me is missing. Sometimes the loneliness for him just engulfs me.

But through it all, God has been right there and has done some wonderful things for me that have made everything bearable.

I can testify that with God all things are indeed possible. (See Mark 10:27.) As you are in the midst of your own struggles, you are in the palm of God's hand. Even when everything in you tells you to run, to be afraid, to turn away, don't listen to your mind. Instead, open your heart and listen with your spirit, for God will indeed speak to you and guide you. He will let you know that He is with you. He has not forsaken you. And everything that concerns you is in His care, shielded by His love.

Remember, too, what I said about faith being a journey that is different for all of us. God has blessed me with what I have needed, and He knew that I would share it. That is part of His plan for me. It will be different for you. He reveals Himself to different people in different ways. For example, Dennis's mother keeps waiting for a sign and wonders why she doesn't experience some of the things that Chase and I do. For me, experiencing God in these unique ways happened when I gave up control and trusted in God totally. I made the choice and I let go of everything. And I *believed.* Since that moment, everything changed.

I understand that giving up control and believing in Someone that we can't see is very difficult. I hope that my story will touch your heart, strengthen your faith and lead you closer to God. I know that God wants you to know Him in more intimate ways than ever before. So from here on, I encourage you to take the blinders from your natural eyes and listen to God's calling to your spirit.

## God's Help Through Transition

During the last several months, God has given me so many blessings and messages that I almost don't know where to begin telling about them. I guess the best place to start is with Dennis himself.

God allowed Dennis to be with me in those first several days. From the day I found out that he was gone to the day we buried his body, I could feel Dennis with me. It's very hard to describe; it was not like depictions in the movies where people hear a disembodied voice or feel someone next to them. What you feel is the person's spirit—their familiar essence—and a sense of love and peace.

A childhood friend, Liz, and I had a similar experience years earlier when another friend passed away. Leslie was only thirteen. I was in ninth grade and Liz was in tenth. The evening after Leslie's funeral, as I was lying on my bed in the dark and crying, I suddenly felt a sense of peace and heard Leslie say to me, "Don't cry, Cathy. I'm fine."

I didn't tell any of my friends about this experience. And it wasn't until almost twenty years later, while visiting Liz in her home, that she confessed that there was something she had never told me. To my surprise, she reported going home the night after Leslie's funeral and, as she lay there crying, hearing Leslie tell her the same thing she told me—not to cry, that she was OK. I'm not sure why God let Leslie talk to Liz and me the night after her funeral; I think, for me, it was so that, when the time came, I would recognize that Dennis was really with me and I wasn't making it up to console myself.

During those first few days, I heard Dennis saying little things to me as I walked through the house. He joked or teased me like he always had. (Once, when I was feeling his loss particularly deeply, he held my face in his hands, looked into my eyes, told me he loved me and gave me a soulful kiss. I believe this happened so that I would know, without a doubt, that he loved me and always will. Though this particular episode might sound crazy, it is the only way I can describe my experience. To truly understand what I am saying, you would have to experience it yourself.) During those few days, his little comments and "Dennis-ness," brought real comfort. In His tender mercy and love, God allowed Dennis to help me transition into being without the physical presence of my husband.

## He Was There to Calm Me

If you have never been through this experience this may not seem like a big deal, but I had to pick out the clothes that Dennis would be buried in. It was a deeply personal and very difficult job. It was also something that I knew I had to do alone.

I put off this task until the night before I was to take the clothes to the funeral home. The house was quiet. Other family members were gone and only my best friend, Sharon, was in the house with me. She was in the guest room on the other side of the house and Chase was asleep on my bed. As I was considering what shirt to choose, I kept coming back to one of his favorites—the shirt he had worn the day Chase was born. He looked really good in that shirt, and it was always one of my favorites on him. When I finally decided on the shirt, I heard Dennis say, "Yeah, that's a good one." He was there with me and I didn't feel so alone anymore. From the mirth in his voice, I could tell that it was the same old Dennis and he was enjoying helping me pick out his clothes. That lightened the tension that had been building in me. There was still a connection between us, although he wasn't physically with me anymore. That comfort gave me strength to go on.

I knew that I should pick khaki pants for him to wear, but I wasn't sure which pair would be best. Dennis had about six different pairs that were usually folded and stacked neatly on the shelf in his closet. I remember half-heartedly thinking, *I guess any pair will do.* But when I opened his closet, only one pair of khaki pants was on the shelf in front of me. As I pulled them down, I thought, *I guess these will do.* When I unfolded them, I saw that they were his cargo pants. I had forgotten he had cargo pants; but as soon as I saw them, I knew they were the right pants. They had been his favorite pants, and he had even bought Chase a pair just like them.

As I was ironing the pants, I had to smile when I heard him giving me a hard time—as he always did—and saying, "Don't forget the creases." I could feel him right beside me, looking over my shoulder. This reminded me of how just hearing his voice calmed me down on our wedding day. Even though we weren't getting married until 6:00 P.M., I had woken up around 6:00 A.M. with butterflies in my stomach. I couldn't sleep, but I didn't want to get up either. So I just lay there for about an hour, until he called me. The instant I heard his voice, everything was OK. It seemed like something washed over me and I knew that everything was right, that it was as it should be. That's how I felt when I was ironing his pants. He was there with me, calming me down so that I could go on. The anxiety and fear that kept trying to creep in were washed away. That was just one of the ways God blessed me during this difficult time.

### *The Rings*

The rings were another blessing. The day we found out about Dennis, everything was a jumble and I couldn't think. My dad was coordinating details with Dennis's oldest brother, David, and various other people. When it clicked through my haze, I tearfully told my dad to make sure they got Dennis's keys. This was important to me because Dennis had a habit of putting his wedding ring on his key chain when he played softball or golf. I knew he had probably forgotten to put it back on his finger, because he had just played in a golf tournament that Friday.

I also wanted them to look for his Virginia Military Institute ring, because somehow I knew that Dennis had taken it with him. It had been his dad's ring and was very special to Dennis. Like his father, Dennis had graduated from VMI, but he had lost his own ring a few months after he graduated. When his dad passed away, he left his VMI ring to Dennis. Dennis cleaned it up and wore it often. He also took it on trips with him. He used to proudly show it to Chase, and he planned to give it to him one day.

Dennis's brothers, David and Dan, and his brother-in-law Chris went up to Tallahassee the day after we found out about the accident. They wanted to see the site of the accident, talk to the police and hospital staff, and get Dennis's belongings.

Chris called me that afternoon and said, "Cathy, are you sure the VMI ring isn't there at the house? We can't find it. We've looked everywhere and it's not here."

I knew it wasn't at the house, but I looked anyway. When I told Chris that it wasn't there, he said they would keep looking. My dad had already told me that they had Dennis's wedding band and that it had been right where I said it would be: on his key chain. But I was worried about the VMI ring because I knew how special it was and how much Dennis wanted Chase to have it.

I didn't talk to them again until David came over the next day with Dennis's belongings. I'll never forget the way he looked as he walked through the front door with Dennis's travel bag. It was so ceremonious. I thought it would be hard to see Dennis's things or to receive them, but it was actually a comfort. After taking the bag into the bedroom for me, David stood looking at me for a minute and then handed me both rings. He told me that they had looked everywhere for the VMI ring. They had looked through all of Dennis's luggage and belongings, they had combed the accident site, and they had had people look through the car. No one had been able to find it.

But then when they returned to the accident site one last time, David had stood there and said, "Den, show me where the ring is." He said something told him to go over and look in Dennis's shaving kit. Dan said he'd already looked all through it and the ring wasn't there. But this time, when David unzipped the side pocket, there was the ring!

I took the VMI ring and put it in a cedar box on top of the dresser, along with Dennis's watch and his wallet. I had owned the box for quite a while, but never knew what to put in it. That day I knew that it was for Dennis's things. I put his wedding band on the chain I wear around my neck, next to my cross. I will never take it off.

That day David also told me a little about the accident. I didn't want to know a lot of the details, but I did want to know the basics. Evidently, Dennis's colleague, John, lived about an hour outside of Tallahassee. When Dennis left his house that night, he went north, instead of south, on the highway that leads back into the city. Evidently realizing that he was going in the wrong direction, he had turned onto a dark, desolate county road to go back. At one point, just before the top of a hill, the road curved sharply. There were no signs, no lights, and the speed limit is 55 m.p.h. Dennis simply didn't make the curve and his Nissan Pathfinder hit some pine trees. The accident wasn't discovered until early afternoon the following day. From the extent of his injuries, investigators determined that he had died instantly. His death certificate says that the cause of death was an open head wound. Interestingly, it lists the time of death as "unknown."

## GOD'S TIMING

Thinking about the accident itself is utterly horrifying. Each time my mind starts going there, I remind myself that Dennis didn't experience it; his body did. In accidents like this, God takes us instantly. But in this case, God did something even more wonderful. God has blessed me and cared for me by giving me the knowledge that He took Dennis out of the Pathfinder *before it ever went off the road.*

I was either in my bedroom or my bathroom when the understanding came. It must have been after I gave everything over to God. In an instant, somehow I just knew that Dennis—his spirit and soul—wasn't in the car when it went off the road. But I tabled the thought. Somewhere in my spirit I knew it was true, but outwardly I wondered whether I was just trying to make myself feel better or to block the horror of the accident. I didn't tell anyone about it, not even my mom. Then God, in His glory, confirmed it for me. This confirmation was the third one I mentioned earlier.

## TAKEN RIGHT TO HEAVEN

We had the visitation at the funeral home for Dennis on Sunday, the day before Memorial Day. His memorial service was at our church on Memorial Day. Kim Baker said she would sing *The Lord's Prayer* at the service.

Because everyone had been so touched when she had sang this song at our wedding, it seemed right to have her sing it at Dennis's memorial service—especially since she has a close relationship with God and He works through her so powerfully.

Kim was at the visitation. Just as she was about to leave, Mom brought her over so I could speak to her and thank her for agreeing to sing. I'd been busy talking to a steady stream of people who had come to pay their respects—Dad said that more than 170 people had come that afternoon. After Kim offered her condolences and said she had been praying for us, she sort of smiled and said that the Lord had spoken to her. She said God had told her that He had taken Dennis out of the car before it went off the road. She said that Dennis had been translated right up to heaven and was in the presence of God.

As she told me this, I had to fight back the tears. I don't understand the full implications, but I do know that God wanted me to know this for a reason; partly to emphasize that this situation was a part of His plan—that it had all happened exactly the way He wanted it to—and partly so that people would believe.

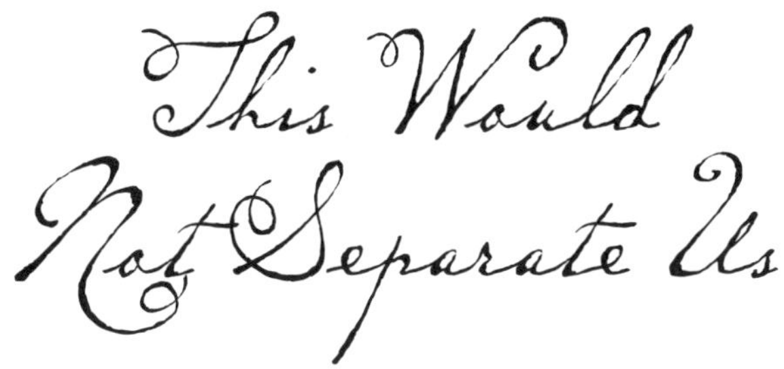


*Blessed is the man who perseveres under trial, because when he has stood the test, he will receive the crown of life that God has promised to those who love him.*

—James 1:12, NIV

Although I have been telling you about how God has comforted me during this time, I want to again emphasize that the grief and pain of my loss have not been taken away. However, these slivers of understanding have made the pain more bearable and have helped me to understand that I can get through anything with God's help. He never promises to take away the pain, but He does promise to help us get through it.

Although I knew Dennis was in heaven, and although

I was tremendously comforted by experiencing his spiritual presence at times, this didn't erase the devastating reality of his loss. The day we had to go to the funeral home to make the arrangements, I alternated between numbness, peace and feeling like I would crumble. Dennis's mother, Lydia, and Susan (David's wife), were going over to go to the funeral home with Dad and me. My mom and my friends, Sharon and Ann, were at my house. People kept coming by to drop off food. Dan's wife, Jenny, also came over with their two girls, Sydney and Avery. Avery was born three days before Chase. We thought it would be good for Chase to play with his cousins.

I wasn't sure what I was feeling as Dad drove us to the funeral home. It wasn't far from my house, so I had passed it many times. Then, while we were looking at pictures of the different caskets we had to choose from, I heard Dennis gently teasing me, saying, "I knew you wouldn't do it." He had always jokingly told me that he wanted to be cremated when he died and have his best friend, Toby, snowboard down from the top of a mountain, scattering his ashes. I think he said it mainly to rile me up; he knew that I would never do it. Reminding me of those conversations was his way of calming me down. He was letting me know that these were just arrangements, and the funeral would not take him away from me. He would always be with me.

As we were sitting in a room and reviewing the options, the funeral director came in to tell us that we would not be able to see Dennis's body, or view it during the funeral. That cut both Lydia and me to the core—but for different reasons. It hurt her to know that she wouldn't be able to get the closure she needed. It hurt me because I instantly knew that the officials in Tallahassee had told him that the accident had been really bad.

Just then, the Holy Spirit gently reminded me that the part that made him Dennis wasn't in the car and that I shouldn't focus on the accident. In retrospect, for several reasons, I'm glad we had the casket closed. First, I didn't want Chase to see his dad like that. But also, I think having it closed kept people from focusing on Dennis's injured body and made it easier for them to believe that he was indeed in heaven. It made it easier to celebrate his life on earth and in heaven.

## WEATHERING ANOTHER STORM WITH GOD'S HELP

Nevertheless, when we first found out we had to keep the casket closed, it hurt terribly. I wanted to scream. I did break down and cry, but in a controlled and respectable way. Inside, though, I could feel the screams raging. I felt like I couldn't breathe. I just wanted to get out of the room. As we drove home, I understood what a caged wild animal must feel like. All I wanted to do was break free and get away from everything and everyone and scream until I couldn't scream any more.

When I walked into my house, I couldn't say anything or look at anyone. I didn't want to stop moving and I didn't want anyone to talk to me. It was as if I was using every ounce of energy I had to hold myself together, and speaking to anyone or looking at anyone would be more than I could bear; I would shatter. When my mom tried to hug me, I shrugged her off and went straight out into the backyard. It was a beautiful afternoon. Impulsively, I climbed up on the trampoline and jumped. I jumped and jumped and jumped. Then I lay down on the trampoline, looked up at the sky and wondered how I could possibly handle what was coming. I prayed for God to help me and give me strength. I knew everyone inside was worried about me—and probably thought I was crazy for jumping on the trampoline. But I just lay there on my back. Soon, I felt some degree of peace. With God's help, I had weathered another storm. I felt a bit stronger and knew that I could go on.

## Tiredness Sets In

What grief does to people is truly incredible. In some respects we go on autopilot, but in other areas grief manifests itself differently at different points of the process. For me, when the shock and numbness began wearing off, tiredness set in. It wasn't really because of lack of sleep. It's true that I didn't really sleep the first night, or maybe even the second; but after that I had no problem sleeping. Even so, my tiredness was like nothing I had ever experienced. I think it resulted from expending so much energy and will power trying to hold myself together so that I didn't shatter into a thousand pieces.

The tiredness really began to hit me on Friday afternoon, when Sharon and I were at the mall looking for something for me to wear to the services that were coming up that weekend. When we were at Dennis's father's funeral a few months earlier, Dennis had told me that I needed to get a new black dress, because the one I was wearing looked like it was stuck in the eighties. So I went out to get clothes, even though I really didn't feel like going.

While shopping, I was so overwhelmed by fatigue and sleepiness that I felt like lying down on the floor and sleeping for days. I felt the same way when I went to the mall the next day with Sharon, Susan and Jenny. I kept sitting down because I didn't think I could go any farther. And to make matters worse, every time I saw a policeman—which happened three or four times that day—my mind flashed back to when the police had come to my house. Each time, my stomach dropped and I felt like someone was twisting a knife in it. Of course, I kept all of this to myself—which drained me of even more energy.

# Waves of Comfort

*Blessed be the God and Father of our Lord Jesus Christ, the Father of mercies and God of all comfort, who comforts us in all our tribulation, that we may be able to comfort those who are in any trouble, with the comfort which we ourselves are comforted by God.*

—2 CORINTHIANS 1:3–4

I am truly overwhelmed when I think about all of the ways God has comforted me and shown me His love and mercy. I have already told you about the first and third ways God showed me that Dennis is heaven, but I have not told you of the second way. In fact, as I explain, I think you will understand why I consider this second confirmation to be pure "gravy."

When God first told me Dennis was in heaven by speaking to me directly and then confirming the revelation through my mom, He was removing any doubt I may have had about Dennis's final destiny. Then the third way He revealed Dennis was in heaven was by telling me that Dennis had actually been translated to heaven before the car even went off the road and then confirming it through the woman who was to sing at the service. The third way helped me combat a specific fear and stay focused on God and His mercy.

## God Speaks Through a Friend

The second way, however, seems to be solely for the purpose of God expressing His love for me. The Friday before the services, I asked my mom to call our hairdresser, Michael, and request that he come to her house that night to touch up my hair. I knew that Michael's visit would take awhile, so I asked Dad to take Chase back to my house.

Shortly after Michael's arrival, he went back out to his car to get something. When he came back in, he asked me if Dennis was 26. I said no, Dennis was 33. Looking puzzled, Michael asked, "Well, you didn't meet when you or he were 26, did you?" I told him no, and he dropped the subject.

I kept thinking about it, though. Later, Michael felt the presence of God and said that God told him to tell me, "Catherine, he is with Me. He has known Me since he was 26." Tears filled my eyes as it suddenly clicked: Dennis was 26 when we married.

Hearing those words, I knew that God was in control and that I would be OK. It also reaffirmed what I think I've known all along—that I now have work to do for the Lord. I've always felt that I would be called to do something for Him, but I never knew what. Actually, I'm still not sure exactly what it is, but I know that it has something to do with writing. So, if the words I have written speak to someone's heart, then know that it is God in His mercy and glory speaking through me.

## ANGELIC VISITATION

You know, God does that. He works through other people. In fact, over and over, I have seen the Lord working through people who have poured out support and compassion for Chase and me. But before I get to that, I'd like to tell you about the angel.

Did you know that God sends His angels in many different forms? I don't know a lot about angels, but I do know there are different kinds. Sometimes, He sends them in human form. Actually, many of us have angelic encounters, but are unaware of them; or, if we suspect that they are angelic, we brush them off as "nonsense." I guess we assume our encounters couldn't possibly be with angels, because we are so focused on this temporal world—on "reality" and "facts" as we know them.

Some of us simply cannot handle the reality of the spiritual realm, especially if we haven't yet realized that God will speak to us, or that He would actually do miracles in our day.

Anyway, the Tuesday that Dennis went to

Tallahassee, I had our regular pest control service scheduled. We usually have the same person come out on calls, but that day I didn't recognize the person who came. Actually, by the time he arrived, I was starting to get a little annoyed because he was about 45 minutes late. Finally the doorbell rang, and when I opened the door, a gentle, black man was standing there.

He apologized for being late, and almost immediately any annoyance I had been feeling disappeared. There was something about him that was very calming. He had the most soulful eyes. Other than just feeling the calmness, I didn't think much about him when he was there. I didn't have time to give him much notice, because my hands were full with being on a conference call and keeping track of Chase.

I did think it was a bit unusual when I noticed him looking around as he walked through my kitchen, talking in a low voice. The only words I could make out were "Praise Jesus." I was a little surprised—but in a pleasant way. Again, somehow, I just felt comfortable having him in the house.

I kept thinking that I needed to remind him to take the small spray canister he had set on my kitchen counter. When it was time for me to pay for the service, I reminded him of the canister and brought it over to him so he wouldn't forget it. I wanted to put the fee on my credit card, but when he tried to call the charge in, he told me that he was having a bit of a problem with the procedure. He apologized, and said that he had never handled a credit payment before. I knew the problem couldn't be with my credit card, because the balance on the account was zero.

Then, when he told me that they were asking for his employee identification number and he didn't have it with him, I said I would just write a check. I didn't want to hold him up any longer, because I'd heard him say he was late for his next appointment. He sure seemed to be taking his time, though.

Finally he looked at me and said, "The fleas are really bothering her."

When I looked at him in a puzzled way, he said, "The cat."

Then he told me about some flea stuff that his boys used on their dog. I was a little bewildered, because I didn't remember him seeing our cat, Sasha. But because I already knew that the fleas had been bothering her, I sort of shrugged off his comment. What resonated with me, though, was the depth of caring in his voice. I guess I was preoccupied with the cat conversation, because when I walked back into the house after he left, I saw that he had forgotten the canister. I contemplated calling the company to let them know that he had left it, but then I remembered that I was having a termite inspection the next day. I decided just to give the canister to the termite guy to take back to their office.

But that was not the last time I saw the pest control man. On the Friday morning after the accident, my doorbell rang. When I opened the door, there he stood. He just looked at me with those eyes; they were so gentle, and yet they seemed to look right through me. As this man and I were locked in a stare, I felt a strong sense of anticipation. But then my parents drove up and began getting out of the car with their arms full of things to bring into the house. In response to the interruption, the man asked me if he had left the canister. I explained that I had given it to the termite man and asked him if he wanted to know the man's name. When he said yes, I located the receipt for the termite inspection and told him the name. He just looked at me and started talking in such a low tone that I couldn't make out what he was saying.

He said something about not seeing it all the first time he was there, that he had seen it when he walked up and noticed Chase's bench. (It is engraved with the words "Jesus Loves Me.")

Suddenly, he looked me in the face and point blank asked me, "Do you know Jesus?"

Without hesitation, I said, "Yes."

Then I told him that I had just lost my husband...on Tuesday night, in fact.

He praised Jesus again and said something I couldn't understand. Then he said, "I think that's why I was supposed to come here. Everything will be OK. You know that he is with the Lord."

When I told him that I knew that, he looked at me and said, "I'll pray for you. We will always be friends."

Then he left.

Even then, I had a feeling that he was an angel. I wasn't sure though, and I thought I might just be desperately trying to see divine things everywhere. But a week or so after

I got back from burying Dennis, I had to call for another pest control service visit because carpenter ants were invading my porch. I wondered if I would see that same man again. In the two years that we've had the service, the same person would always return, unless that person left the company or had been promoted. However, my friend didn't return. I was surprised to see a different man standing at the door that day instead...one who continued to service our house from that point forward. Somehow I knew in my heart that God had visited me through the man who had praised Jesus throughout my house immediately before and immediately after I had suffered the loss of my husband.

## LIGHT IN THE DARKNESS

In church, I've always heard that we should be a light for Christ, to let His light shine through us. During the days and weeks following Dennis's passing, I've had a strong feeling that God wants us to know that He is the Light, and in Him there is no darkness, as 1 John 1:5 tells us. I believe there are three parts to His message for us. I can't tell you why, but I know the first part has to do with light.

There has been so much darkness in our world. But that darkness is coming to an end. In many ways, God will be shining His light through the darkness and we will be responsible for seeking that light.

We tend to forget how much goodness there is in the world and how good people can be. I have been utterly humbled at the love for Chase and me that has been expressed through others. I have witnessed firsthand how God's light shines through others.

I knew my close friends would be there for me, and they were. In fact, more than I could ever have imagined. But I was also deeply touched by the way people I barely knew, or didn't know at all, showed compassion. Neighbors that I had never met brought by food, flowers and cards—and even toys for Chase. People that I knew professionally came to Dennis's visitation or to the memorial service. Friends that I had grown up with and hadn't seen in years drove to be there for me. Even as I write this, I weep at their compassion.

I think the most compassion has been shown for Chase. Several people asked if we were setting up an education fund for him so they could send money instead of, or even in addition to, flowers. Dennis and I had started a college fund for him, so my dad and my godfather called my broker to see how others could contribute directly to the fund. When the broker called back, he even suggested a newly available fund with more advantages than the original one. The idea was spread by word of mouth and the information we provided in the funeral notice. Although the contributions have been overwhelming, the amount does not matter to me. I am simply humbled by the fact that all of these people cared enough to send something. In the month following Dennis's passing, the contributions to the fund were so generous that Chase will never have to worry about money for college.

That fund is yet another way that God has blessed us.

The donors have also been blessed in their giving. I believe that as God moves in and through the hearts of people, a further awakening to His light—and piercing of darkness—occurs.

# Celebrating Dennis's Earthly and Heavenly Life

When we were planning Dennis's memorial service, I wanted to make sure that we celebrated his life. Dennis had always told me (seriously, by the way) that when he died, he did not want some tearful, mournful service that focused on his death. Instead, he wanted his life to be celebrated. In addition to celebrating his life here on earth, I wanted to make sure that everyone got the message that Dennis may be gone from this world, but he is not dead. I wanted them to realize that, because Dennis is alive in heaven, we should praise God—even during our time of sorrow over the fact that Dennis is not with us in the physical sense.

I've had a lot of people tell me that the memorial service and the visitation were the most beautiful they have ever attended. Everything felt right to me.

As I mentioned earlier, we had the visitation the day before the memorial service. To celebrate his life on earth, we displayed enlarged photos mounted on boards, framed pictures and a framed poem I had written for him. To truly highlight his life, we brought in his two snowboards, his VMI yearbook and hat, his golf clubs, his softball shirt from the church team and his favorite "TEI" shirt. When all of this was put together with the many beautiful flowers and plants, the result was truly peaceful and beautiful. Many people told me afterwards that even though they hadn't known Dennis well, they now had a wonderful sense of his life and what he was like.

## "These Are For You," He Told Me

I think Dennis approved. I could feel him there with me that day. Before the service that morning, when I dropped off his snowboards and other items, I was taken aback when I saw all of the flowers. The bouquets had been arranged on tiered risers and tables and across the floor, filling the room with fragrance and a splendid array of colors. Slowly walking through the room, I looked at the flowers and plants and read the cards. As I was thinking how beautiful they all were, I could hear Dennis say, "There you go, honey; these are for you."

It was like he had been walking right next to me and had gently leaned over my shoulder and whispered those sweet words in my ear. When I heard those words, my heart was washed with a sense of peace—and I didn't feel alone.

## Poems of Love

In the days leading up to the memorial service, I kept trying to figure out what to say at the service. I prayed for God to give me the right words. I wanted them to be His words; words that would touch people and help them to know His presence and His glory.

I kept thinking that I should read something that I had written for Dennis. A few weeks earlier, when we were cleaning out our drawers because we were getting new furniture, Dennis came across a card I had given him for Valentine's Day about three years before. I had always thought it was sort of odd that his sock drawer was where he kept special cards and other things I'd given him. But, that was just Dennis and it was one of those quirks that I loved about him.

When he pulled out the card and read aloud what I had written about how much I loved and appreciated him, I started crying. My tears were for all of the missed opportunities—all of the days gone by when I could have told him those things but didn't. Like so many other people, we had gotten too busy and had taken a lot for granted. Right then, I had promised myself that I would be more loving on a regular basis.

Knowing he had me, he sort of smiled and said that he was going to be sure to hold on to that card, so he could pull it out from time to time and remind me of how wonderful I thought he was.

When I was pondering what to share at the service, I remembered that card. I got up very early one morning and began looking for it, because I thought reading part of what I had written in it would be a good idea. We hadn't finished putting his stuff in the drawers of our new furniture, so I knew the card wouldn't be in his sock drawer.

I searched everywhere for it. Finally, I started looking through the box where we had put stuff from the nightstand. In the box, I found a poem that I had written him for his thirtieth birthday. I had completely forgotten about it. As I read it, I knew this was one of the things I wanted to share at the service. It felt right. I had written the poem on the computer, and printed it out on our printer; but across the top of the paper I had handwritten, "Den, this is for you on your 30th birthday. Love, Cathy."

To help you understand a little more about Dennis and me—and our relationship—I want to share this poem with you:

# You and I

*You and I are all I know,*
*Growing, changing as we go.*
*You and I, the best of friends,*
*Start to finish, beginning to end.*
*You and I are like a song,*
*A melody that drifts along.*
*You and I are like the wind,*
*Raging fierce, then soft again.*
*You and I are partners true,*
*Separate but equal in all we do.*
*You and I, a puzzle grand,*
*Together a whole, hand in hand.*
*You and I are like a fire,*
*A steady burning warm desire.*
*You and I are like the rain,*
*Gently washing away the pain.*
*You and I, a rainbow bright,*
*Colors blended by the light.*
*You and I go on and on,*
*Growing closer with each new dawn.*
*You and I, our love is true,*
*That's why I give my heart to you.*

# Purified Love

I've been reading a few things lately, and bits of information stick out for me. I was in the shower the other day when suddenly pieces of a puzzle began falling together in my mind, and I had a revelation. It started with something that Martha Whitmore Hickman wrote in the introduction to her book, *Healing After Loss: Daily Meditations for Working Through Grief*. When my sister-in-law Susan gave me the book, I glanced through it but didn't feel that it was for me. But when my dad found it on the table and read some of it, he said that it helped him. Later I picked it up again and several things in the introduction resonated within me, particularly the statement, "...in addition to the poignancy of loss comes the rush of love for the one we have lost and perhaps a sense that in the mystery of the universe, we will inhabit that universe together and are tied together in a love that cannot come untied."[1]

This is how I feel about Dennis; as if our marriage has forever been sealed and we are bound together for eternity. But the most wonderful part is the rush of love. It is as though all of the past annoyances and grievances, all of the worldly things, have been washed away—and all that is left is pure love. Then I remembered the words of Max Lucado, in his book *When Christ Comes,* who says that when we die in Christ our clothing in heaven becomes spotless. All of the sin, the jealousies, the pettiness, all of the less-than-pure characteristics and qualities are washed away and all that is left is the goodness and the love.[2] This happens because Christ exchanges all of our sin for what is referred to in the Bible as "garments of salvation." (See Isaiah 61:10.) So, as I stood there in the shower, I realized that the reason I have felt this pure bond on our marriage and the rush of pure love is because Dennis has indeed become washed clean by Christ. All of the imperfections are gone. The Dennis that I feel and I now know, is the pure one who is in heaven. It is an absolutely amazing feeling. It is also further proof to me of God's grace and glory.

## You Can Let Go of the Burden

OK; you may be saying, "If that's the case, why haven't I felt that for my loved one? Why are so many people left with negative feelings, or feeling that there is something unresolved? Why do they have the torment, and why does peace elude them?"

Only God can answer those questions, and the answer

is probably different for each person. Maybe their loved one didn't know the Lord, or maybe they themselves refuse the Lord, so somewhere inside they know that they will never see them again. But I think that, for most people, it comes down to the fact that they can't completely let go and put everything in God's hands. They hold on to what their minds can relate to more easily—to death—and they clutch the burden like a badge they think they must wear.

Actually, it's hard to avoid focusing on the death part. After all, it's something that has happened through the ages, and the reality that resonates the most is that the person is not here anymore. So, many people can't get past it. It's hard for them to believe that death is not final. Why is it that no one questions the miracle of birth, but there are so many questions about death? Why is it so hard to believe that the God who breathes life into us could give us something more?

## God Woos Me Back to Himself

When we lose someone we love, the grief and sense of loss are so enormous that it is almost unbearable. Most people get trapped there because they focus on the death of the earthly body. When they do, they are overwhelmed by a sense of finality. That's when the doubt, anger, depression, fear, unforgiveness and other darkness attacks—and that's exactly what it is, an attack.

This attack comes directly from great deceiver. Satan's plot is for the person who has experienced loss to feel and be trapped by overwhelming, negative emotions.

The purpose of this sabotage is to direct a person's focus away from the glory of God and the salvation that we all have, if we accept Christ as our personal Savior.

We must keep in mind, however, that accepting Christ as Savior is only the first step. God doesn't impose on us. He usually waits for us to ask Him for what we need, or for us just to seek Him even if we don't know what it is that we need. To get past all the darkness, we must turn everything over to God and trust that He will guide us. We also have to accept that what we want or when we want it may not be in His plan for us. I think that accepting His plan is one of the hardest things to do. When I have struggled with this—and even in my everyday life—the scripture that I have always leaned on discusses this very point:

> *Trust in the Lord with all your heart, and lean not on your own understanding; in all your ways acknowledge Him, and He shall direct your paths.*
>
> —PROVERBS 3:5–6

It's also amazing to realize that God truly never leaves us. We may try to leave Him, but He will not leave us. Three months after losing Dennis, I went through a period where the pain was so great, I didn't think I could stand it anymore. Instead of turning to God, I tried to run away from everything. I was completely drained emotionally, I wasn't able to focus on work and I didn't feel like talking to my friends. Because it was too painful, I didn't want to deal with anything that reminded me of

Dennis. I got to the point where I couldn't even look at his picture. I would weakly pray and reach out to God, but then turn away again. I tried to distract myself, but God wouldn't let go of me. Finally, I gave it all up to Him again and freely admitted that I was weak and I was running.

As I sat in church praying for God to forgive me and help me, I knew in my heart that I was ready to listen again. Then, as clear as a bell, the Holy Spirit said the words, "Psalm 32."

I opened the Bible and read what that psalm says:

*Blessed is he whose transgression is forgiven,*
*Whose sin is covered.*
*Blessed is the man to whom the Lord does not*
*impute iniquity,*
*And in whose spirit there is no deceit.*

*When I kept silent, my bones grew old*
*Through my groaning all the day long.*
*For day and night Your hand was heavy upon*
*me;*
*My vitality was turned into the drought of*
*summer.*
*I acknowledged my sin to You,*
*And my iniquity I have not hidden.*
*I said, "I will confess my transgressions to the*
*Lord,"*
*And You forgave the iniquity of my sin.*

*For this cause everyone who is godly shall pray to*
*You*
*In a time when You may be found;*
*Surely in a flood of great waters*
*They shall not come near him.*
*You are my hiding place;*
*You shall preserve me from trouble;*
*You shall surround me with songs of*
*deliverance.*

*I will instruct you and teach you in the way you*
*should go;*
*I will guide you with My eye.*
*Do not be like the horse or like the mule,*
*Which have no understanding,*
*Which must be harnessed with bit and*
*bridle,*
*Else they will not come near you.*
*Many sorrows shall be to the wicked;*
*But he who trusts in the Lord, mercy shall*
*surround him.*

*Be glad in the Lord and rejoice, you righteous;*
*And shout for joy, all you upright in heart!*

Because I was listening to Him again and no longer running from His voice, the Lord was able to comfort me, give me hope and point me to Himself.

# A Son Knows Daddy Is in Heaven

*Blessed are the pure in heart, for they shall see God.*

—Matthew 5:8

Thinking of Chase growing up without Dennis is one of the hardest things for me to deal with. It makes tears well up in my eyes, and it feels like an arrow is piercing me. I think it worries most of our friends and family, too. Dennis was an incredible father and loved Chase with all of his heart; and Chase idolized Dennis. He still talks about how Daddy cut down the tree and how Daddy took him to watch planes.

Chase was in the room with me when I found out about Dennis's accident. I don't know exactly what he heard, because I don't remember myself. But he knew something was wrong. Sending him to my friend Danica's house was a salvation for me, because it gave me time to start dealing with the news without worrying about him watching me fall apart.

I wrestled with what to tell him—and when. I didn't know how much he would understand. I had read that because young children have little sense of permanence, when they lose someone they love, they keep thinking the person will just come back. I had no idea how he would handle it, or whether I would have to keep explaining things to him over and over again. Worst of all, I dreaded the pain and loss he might feel.

## Daddy's Not Coming Back

That first night when we were getting ready to go to sleep, he was still anxious because he knew something was wrong. I didn't bother trying to make him sleep in his bed, but brought him in bed with me. He had always woken up in the middle of the night anyway and would come and get in bed with Dennis and me, so I was just skipping the first part. The few times he woke up that night, he kept feeling on Dennis's side of the bed and calling out "Da Da." Not knowing what to do, I just said, "Daddy's not here, Baby."

The next morning it was quiet and peaceful in Chase's room as I was getting him dressed. The morning light was shining through his window, and I could tell that he was paying attention to me. Kneeling on the floor, I took his little hands in mine and I said very calmly and simply, "Chase, Daddy had to go to heaven. He is in heaven with God and he is OK. But he won't be coming back, so we won't be able to see Daddy anymore."

He hung his little head down. He was so still, listening to what I said.

I asked him if he was OK. In a small, quiet voice, he said yes.

I pulled him to me and held him in my arms. I had no idea whether he comprehended what I was telling him, but within myself I felt that he did.

The first few days afterward were unsettling for him, because so many people came in and out of the house—and everyone was so sad. For his age, he handled it all very well. He continued feeling for Dennis in bed the second night, each time calling for Da Da; But somewhere in those first few days, something interesting happened. He stopped calling Dennis "Da Da" and started calling him "Daddy."

The day that I made the arrangements at the funeral home, my friend Ann, my mom, my sister-in-law Jenny, and her two girls were all at the house. Both Ann and my mom told me separately about something that happened while I was gone. They had all been in the backyard with Chase when, suddenly, he stopped what he was doing and looked at something that they couldn't see. He looked at my mom with a confused expression and then looked back at the place where he had been looking. Then he said, "Da Da!"

## Answered Prayer

Both Ann and my mom were convinced that he was seeing Dennis at that time. When they told me about it, I had no doubt that he did see Dennis. After all, I was feeling Dennis with me, and I knew firsthand that God is merciful. I had been praying that God would help Chase through this difficult time. I also know that, because they are so new to this world, children are sometimes able to see things in the spiritual realm that adults can't see. Because of this innocence, children's minds don't shut things out like our minds do.

I was grateful that God allowed Chase to see Dennis that afternoon. I kept praying that God Himself would explain things to Chase, and that He would allow Dennis to do the same thing. I prayed that God would tell Chase the real truth and would strengthen him with it. The Friday night before the services, two days after Dennis had passed away, my mother told me that she had been praying the same thing for Chase. Until then, I hadn't mentioned to her that I had been praying for Chase in this way, but when she told me this, I knew in my heart that God would answer our prayers. And He did!

In fact, God has done some absolutely amazing things for Chase. One morning, after praying for Chase the night before, I woke up before Chase did. I hadn't slept well, but Chase was smiling in his sleep. Later, as we were lying in the bed after he woke up, he had such a peaceful look on his face. This was another one of those moments when I knew he was listening to me and wasn't distracted by anything.

I looked at him and said, "Chase, did God talk to you?"

He said, "Yes...Daddy."

I asked, "God talked to you about Daddy?"

"Yes," he replied.

"Are you OK?"

"Yes."

Since then, on several occasions, I have known that Chase has seen Dennis and that God has allowed Dennis to speak with him. I believe that God allowed Dennis to be here at times during this early period, and then eventually Chase started seeing him in heaven. I know this idea may be hard to believe, and that you may even think I am mistaking the imagination of a child for something more. But that is not the case. Other people have witnessed some of this, and it is clear that Chase isn't making things up. I want to stress that Chase is not expecting Dennis to come back, as little ones his age do when they have lost someone. After God spoke to Chase that Friday night, he stopped looking for and calling out for Dennis. Even though he didn't stop thinking about him and talking about him, it was clear that he knew his daddy wasn't coming back.

### *I Miss Daddy, Too*

Either Saturday or Sunday night before the memorial service, Chase and I were lying on the floor in my office and watching a *Blues Clues* video. Sharon was watching television in the den right outside my office, and it reminded me of how Dennis used to sit out there and watch TV while we watched this show in my office. I imagined Dennis coming in to check on us, as he usually did. Evidently, Chase was thinking the same thing, because he got a sad look on his face and said, "Miss." At first I didn't know what he was talking about, so I asked, "Miss?" Then he said, "Miss Daddy," and turned and buried his little face in my chest. I could just feel the grief in him. I said, "I miss Daddy too, Baby" and just held him as the tears rolled down my face.

That's the thing about Chase. He tells me that he misses Dennis and he tells me that he is sad, but he never ever acts like Dennis is coming back. I think this is quite amazing for a little guy his age. I know the reason he is able to comprehend the situation is because God answered my prayers. I'm certain that God explained the situation to Chase in way that he could understand. I also know that God allowed Chase to see and to talk to Dennis after the accident.

## Daddy's in Heaven!

Chase has told me on several occasions that Dennis is playing golf in heaven. That may sound ridiculous to some people, but I'm sure that he is. God gives us the desires of our hearts in heaven, and I know that Dennis loves playing golf. A day or so after we buried Dennis, Chase stopped what he was doing and looked out the window. What was unusual about this was the way he seemed to actually be looking somewhere else; somewhere beyond where the normal eye can see.

What happened next confirmed that Chase was seeing

beyond the physical realm. After a few seconds of looking out the window in this way, he said, "Daddy."

Sensing how special this moment was, I asked him if he had seen Daddy.

He said, "Yes."

"What is Daddy doing?"

Looking at me somewhat in disbelief, he said, "Golf."

A bit stunned, I asked, "Daddy's playing golf?"

Seeming a little hurt that I doubted him, he quietly said, "Yes."

It was a while before Chase could actually say the word *heaven*. I remember the first time he did though. It was a couple of weeks after the funeral. We had gone out to get the mail, and on the way back up the driveway, Chase suddenly stopped and started looking up toward the tree. Although I assumed that he was looking at the tree, I asked him, "What are you looking at?"

At first, he didn't answer me or even look at me. But then he snapped out of it and said "Daddy."

"Do you see Daddy?"

"Yes."

"Where is Daddy?"

Standing right there in middle of our driveway, Chase threw both arms up, lifted his face toward the sky, and exclaimed, "Heaven!"

The thing that really struck me as interesting was that he was looking up. I knew for a fact that I was the only person who had mentioned heaven to him, and I never said anything about "up in heaven," I always said "in heaven."

## Not Just a Fantasy

As wonderful as these episodes are to share, I don't want you to get the wrong impression and think that Chase is off in fantasyland, thinking that his dad is in heaven. To help you understand, I'd like to restate the fact that even though God has been so good to both of us, the many ways He has comforted us and blessed us haven't taken away the pain and the sense of loss.

The fact that Chase feels the pain and he misses his dad terribly is a clear sign that he is not denying reality and living in a fantasy. The time around the burial was the worst. He had a lot of trouble sleeping at night and would get extremely upset. He wouldn't go in the bedroom at night, so we had to lie on the floor in the living room until he fell asleep watching his favorite video, *Spot*.

During those early days, he frequently woke up crying during the night. At times he was almost inconsolable, and often he insisted that my dad take him outside to look at the moon. Usually, this was the only thing that would come close to calming him down. When my parents told me that they wondered why Chase was fixated on the moon, I explained to them that, after dinner on many nights, Dennis and Chase would go outside and jump on the trampoline—and then they would lie down on it and look up at the moon.

## His Perception Kept Amazing Me

Even shopping without Dennis was hard for Chase. About a month after Dennis passed away, Chase and I went to Target without Dennis for the first time. As we shopped, I thought about how the three of us had always done this together—because it was so difficult to keep Chase in the shopping cart. Realizing how much I was missing Dennis right then, I wondered if Chase was thinking about him, too—but he didn't seem to be at that moment.

Then, when I was letting him play for a few minutes in the front seat of the car before he climbed into his car seat, out of the blue he said, "Miss. Miss Daddy."

Once again, I was amazed by his perception. I knew that he had been thinking about the fact that Dennis wasn't with us at Target.

## One Parent Instead of Two

One Monday was particularly hard for me, because this was the day when it became painfully clear that Chase understood that he no longer had two parents, that in this way he was now different from many other kids. While Chase was napping that day, I called the insurance company to check the status of the claim. It was no big deal, but just talking to them about it really hurt. I pulled myself together on the outside when Chase woke up, because I didn't want to upset him; but on the inside I felt like I was about to crumble.

Then, to make matters worse, Chase and I went out to get the mail and he saw his friend Brian in his front yard with his parents.

Chase kept saying, "Brian, Brian," but I told him that his friend was busy and couldn't play right then. Even after we went into the garage and Chase seemed to be distracted by looking at something, he started saying "Brian" again. He wanted Brian to come and play with him. I bent over to pick up something, and told him again that Brian was busy.

Then it happened.

Chase turned toward me and quietly said, "Parents."

"Yes, Brian is with his parents," I told him.

Sadly, he hung his head and said, "Miss Daddy."

I felt like someone stabbed me. I fell to my knees and started crying.

Not knowing what to do, Chase worriedly said, "Mommy? Mommy?"

I told him that I was sad because I missed Daddy, too. I explained to him that we cry when we're sad. "It's OK to cry and it's OK to miss Daddy…and we will for a long time…"

Chase came closer to me and hugged me. Silently, he held on to me for what seemed like a very long few minutes.

## An Easter Picture for Chase

Something amazing happened on June 27, the Wednesday before we left for St. Simons for our annual Fourth of July week at the beach. Chase had been very sad that day—for two or three days, in fact. Because he was missing Dennis terribly the day before, I had shown him the picture of the three of us that I was planning to hang in his room. It had been taken at Easter and was now enlarged and beautifully mounted. I couldn't help but reflect on how many people at the services had commented on what a great picture it was. Chase was so delighted about the picture that he grabbed it before I could finish pulling it out of the stack.

He ran into his room with it, saying, "Room! Room!" He wanted it in his room. I carefully displayed it on top of his dresser until we could hang it properly. Chase was very excited the next day when my dad hung the picture on the wall for him. After he and Dad left the room, I stumbled on a quiet moment of reflection. I was just about to leave the room myself when I noticed the basket of Easter eggs in the picture. My immediate thought was, *How appropriate!*

As I pondered the beautiful meaning of Easter, of resurrection and new life, I knew that it was the right picture for Chase.

### *Heaven is a Pretty Place*

That Wednesday night as Chase was just finishing up his bath, he told me that he was ready to get out of the tub. I got his towel and was sitting there waiting for him to stand up, when he got very quiet. When I told him I was ready for him to get out, I realized that his mind was elsewhere. I sat and watched for a moment, until he abruptly snapped out of it. I was a bit startled by his sudden burst of excitement and joy when his whole face lit up and he said, "Daddy!"

Inquiring, I said, "Daddy?"

"Daddy! Heaven!" he responded.

Thinking I knew what he was saying, I said, "Yes, Daddy's in heaven."

Not satisfied that I understood all that he meant, he looked at me hard and said, "No, Daddy in HEAVEN!" I could tell that he suddenly understood what heaven was, because he had seen it.

I asked him if he saw Daddy in heaven and he said yes.

"What does heaven look like?"

Looking at me with wonder and joy, he said, "Oh, *pretty! Pretty!*"

Then he became a little frustrated when he said some other words, but I didn't understand what he was trying to tell me. He wanted to explain, but he didn't know how. He kept saying "wrapped." But at the time I didn't know what that meant. I later came to understand that when Chase saw Dennis in heaven he was wrapped in some type of garment.

"Did Daddy say something to you?"

"Yes."

"What did Daddy say to you?"

Silence.

"Did you see anyone else?"

Reverently, he said, "God."

"Did God say anything to you?"

"Yes."

"What did God say?"

Chase looked up at me with joy and said, "Picked Daddy."

My heart filled with overflowing joy and I blurted out the question, "God told you that He picked Daddy?"

Chase said, "Yes."

"Does that make you happy?"

As he smiled and said yes, the look on his face seemed to say that God had shared some wonderful secret with Chase that had filled his heart with such joy and excitement that it was spilling over. I was so grateful, I couldn't do anything but praise the Lord for blessing both of us in such a tender and miraculous way.

## Confirmations That We Will See Dennis Again

I don't know what Dennis told Chase or what else God shared with him, but Chase has given me some clues. On two occasions he has hinted at this in the same way. The first hint came a day or so after he told me he had seen Daddy and God in heaven. The second came when were driving to St. Simons with my dad.

Both times, out of the blue, he simply said, "Daddy. Coming."

Both times when I said, "Daddy's coming?" he said "Yes. Eggs."

The moment he said "eggs" I knew in my spirit that he was talking about the Resurrection. This confirmed to me what I had been thinking that day when I stood alone in Chase's room, looking at the Easter picture. Jesus had confirmed to Chase, and to me, that we will see Dennis again on the day of Resurrection.

## More Hints About Heaven

Before I get to the second part of what I refer to as "the bathtub message," I want to share some other things that Chase has experienced. One morning he woke up and was happily saying "Daddy." I asked if he had seen Dennis and he said yes. So I asked him where he saw Dennis and, as usual, he told me "heaven."

I said, "What was it like?" and he said, "Window." Puzzled, I said, "Window?" and he said, "Yes. Window open."

"It was like a window opening?"

"Yes. Chase. Through. In."

"You went through the window into heaven?"

"Yes."

Then he didn't want to talk about it anymore.

On another occasion, again while he was in the bathtub, Chase told me how he'd seen Dennis in heaven. He started talking about "Daddy's house" and told me it was blue. I asked him where Daddy's house was, and he said it was in heaven. Motioning that it was somewhere else, he said it was "over." Again, he told me about going through "the window."

He's referred to the window several other times. When he does, he's not talking about a window in our house. I understand that he is referring to a window into heaven, because whenever I ask him about it, he refers to it as "over."

As a matter of fact, about the time he started talking about going through the window into heaven, he was taking three-hour naps during the day. I started to suspect that he was sleeping so long because God was taking him to heaven then. That was later confirmed for me.

## CHASE RECOGNIZES JESUS

The thing that really amazed me and strengthened my belief that he's not making this up, was when he looked at some Bible Action Cards he got in the mail from The *Beginners Bible*, pointed to a figure and exclaimed, "Jesus!" The cards have cartoon-like illustrations of different people from the Bible, and some of them are hard even for me to recognize. To confirm Chase's ability to recognize a picture of Jesus, I found another card that had the picture of Jesus on it and, after a while, I showed the card to Chase and asked, "Who's this?"

He looked at me as if to say, "DUH!" and said "Jesus." We don't have any pictures of Jesus in our house. Plus, when I had talked to Chase about Daddy being in heaven, I had always said that Daddy was with God—and had not mentioned Jesus. To confirm that his ability to identify Jesus was not the result of his natural childhood experiences, I asked my mom if she had been showing Chase pictures of Jesus. She told me that she intentionally had not shown him any pictures of Jesus and had not talked about Him, because she had been afraid that doing so would have made Chase sad.

A few days later, Chase pointed to the card again and said, "Jesus." I asked him if he'd seen Jesus before, and he said yes.

I asked, "Where did you see Jesus?"

"Heaven." A few other times since then Chase told me that he saw Dennis in heaven and Jesus was there, too.

## More about the Bathtub Message

Now back to the "bathtub message." After the event when Chase was in the tub, on two occasions, Chase spontaneously talked about "Daddy coming" and "eggs." A week or so after saying this, on two different occasions he mentioned yet another message. Both times he broke out in a smile and said, "Waiting." When I asked what he was waiting for, he said, "Daddy." It wasn't as if he expected Dennis to come right then, or to be alive here on earth. He meant that he was waiting for Dennis to come back with Christ.

This message given to—and through—my young son, further confirms that we need to be actively awaiting Christ's return. This revelation meshes with my sense of urgency that God wants us to know that He is real.

All of this started making more sense to me when I read something that the evangelist Jesse Duplantis wrote in his book, *Heaven: Close Encounters of the God Kind.* I had read the book a few years before, but recently I felt compelled to read it again. When I read the following passage, I realized why. In the book, Duplantis describes a revelation that he had about Jesus. I have felt exactly this same way, but he describes it much better than I can.

He writes,

> *But I see that His coming is not just His return, it is the witness of who He is. When He said in the gospels that His kingdom was not of this world, He was trying to get the people to see the witness of who*

> *He is and not just understand the signs that pointed to Him as the Messiah. I felt that He was saying our eyes should be on Him, Jesus, instead of on the great tribulation period.*[3]

## BEING A SHINING LIGHT

Though I didn't need further confirmation, our pastor said something in church one Sunday that resonated with me. He said he had recently explained to a young man at camp that no matter how good or how bad we are, God will always love us just the same. He told the young man that we *cannot* change that fact—no matter what we do. We *can*, however, shine God's light into the world for others to see, so that they may come to know Him. Because He wants others to know Him, we can shine His light by reaching out to others and helping them, trying to follow the example that Christ set for us, and sharing what the Lord has done in our lives. In summary, this is our mission.

Now you understand more clearly why I have shared this portion of my journey with you. I want to share what the Lord has done for me and for my son in our darkest time. This is the time to believe and to really get to know God. He wants us to know Him and to have a relationship with Him.

I sense an urgent call. He is reaching out to us; but in response, we must reach out to Him and desire to know Him. Without a doubt, I can tell you that God is very real and that He loves us. Salvation is indeed available to us through Jesus Christ…and I know of nothing more wonderful.

# Attacks of Doubt and Fear Are Calmed by More Revelation

As I prepared to share this experience in writing with people, I started getting attacked. Satan tried to make me doubt my experiences and to be reluctant to share the glory of God with others. But then, one day when I was entering a particularly rough period, I visited a very anointed friend. During my few hours with Michael, God continually confirmed things and strengthened me in my spirit. I didn't know what was before me, but the Lord did. It was as if He was giving me an infusion of His Spirit because He knew that I was in danger of being sent reeling.

As I talked with Michael, I could feel the presence of the Holy Spirit, as if electricity or energy was going through me. When this happens, sometimes it's just a tingle, but other times it's more powerful.

As I shared with Michael that Chase had told me that

he had seen Dennis and that he had gone through a window into heaven, the power of the Holy Spirit upon me became so great that the sense of electricity flowing through me was incredibly strong. My skin started getting warm and the presence of God upon me became so strong that I felt like I was going to fall out of my chair. As I was speaking, I could tell that Michael felt the presence of God, too, and that God was speaking to him. At first, he closed his eyes and leaned over. Then, after a little while he told me that Chase had indeed been to heaven. The Lord also told Michael to tell me part of what He had spoken to him. As he shared this, I wept. Even now, I still weep when I talk about it or think about it. I asked Michael to write down what the Lord said. He did:

> *I have allowed the child to go through transfiguration. To see Me and feel Me to take a message back. He has spoken to Dennis and I the Lord. I have allowed this for My glory and to remove grief. I always get the glory.*

Later, as I was sharing other things with Michael, I felt the presence of the Holy Spirit again, and could even smell roses. The Holy Spirit has the most beautiful aroma of roses.

I told Michael about God taking Dennis out of the car before it went off the road. He just looked at me like something had clicked, and then told me about a friend of his who had a dream about that very thing. Wouldn't you know, before I left, she called Michael and he asked her to describe her dream to me. A few months earlier she had dreamed she was walking with her friend and a beam of light came down, engulfed her friend, and suddenly her friend was gone. She was wondering what had happened to her friend, but then she vanished, too. In her dream state she wasn't afraid, but she did keep thinking about how her husband and child would miss her. She said she could hear voices all around, and she knew that God was translating people right up to heaven.

Hearing about her dream was added confirmation to me that God did take Dennis out of the car before it went off the road. In fact, I believe the car left the road because God had taken him—had translated him into heaven just as He had shown Michael's friend. That was God's plan. All the glory belongs to Him.

Feeling the presence of God, hearing a message from God through Michael, and the account of this woman's dream were all ways in which God emboldened me to share the details of my journey. Again, the reality of life beyond what we can see and hear with our natural eyes and ears has been confirmed to me over and over. I am responding to God's call for me to share this truth with readers like you.

# God's Power Will Help Us Transcend Some of the Grief

Grief experts commonly preach and counsel about the four stages of grief: shock, denial, anger and resolution. While I'm not denying that most people go through those stages, I don't believe those *have* to be the stages. Actually, I haven't had the denial and anger. Yes, I've felt the anger try to creep in, but it always lifts from me when I pray. The increased discernment that the Lord has blessed me with, has enabled me to recognize that anger and depression are not of Him. He is light and in Him is no darkness at all.

Although I sometimes wonder if the denial and anger will hit me later, the Holy Spirit keeps telling me no. I did experience the shock. Actually, I do think that shock is a necessary part of the process. But, as I have turned everything over to the Lord from the beginning, He has guided me straight from the shock phase into resolution. Why? Because *the resolution is in Him.* And so, while the experts talk about the natural stages of grief, we must keep in mind that what is natural to us is generally of the earth and of humanity. But God is supernatural. And through Him, we can transcend or bypass much of the natural processes that are part of life on earth.

I realize that I am blessed not to have experienced the negative stages of anger and denial. I believe that one reason God has blessed me in that way is so that I could tell others that it is possible.

With God, all things are possible (Mark 10:27). Now, more than ever, it is time to turn to Him rather than lean on our own understanding. Remember, the resolution is in Jesus. He is the ultimate resolution for everything. I encourage those of you who are grieving and struggling to invite Him to be your resolution. Continue to pray for His guidance and for Him to pull you through the tough times. If you do have negative feelings, it does not mean that there is anything wrong with you. While the experience of loss won't be the same for everyone, I do know that the Lord wants us to know that, in Him, we can transcend the depths of grief and even skip part of it altogether.

I am not a licensed counselor, but I am a living witness to what the Lord can do in your life. Ask Him to take charge and to guide you. He may lead you to a counselor or a support group, or whatever it is you need. It is different for each of us. The common factor is that Jesus is there, just waiting for us to ask for His help. It doesn't mean that He will take away all of the struggles or the pain, but He does promise that He will be with us always. He knows our pain and our struggles and He wants to share our burdens.

While the testimony I have shared with you is rooted in a tragedy, I want you to know that you do not have to experience tragedy to really know the Lord or to experience Him. Certainly, an experience like this can bring a person closer to Him, but tragedy is not a requirement.

Thinking about getting closer to the Lord as a continuous journey that is unique to each of us, reminds me of something I heard a conference speaker say recently. The gist of what she said was, "Yes, there are times when I think 'OK, I'll go to bed and then wake up in the morning and be a godly woman.' But it doesn't work like that."

That statement is so true. Getting closer to Jesus—and the transformation that happens in us when we do—doesn't happen overnight. Like any good relationship, developing a closer walk with the Lord takes work…and the desire to make it work. One of the most important things to remember is that God is always there for us, no matter what. First, we must reach out to Him and invite Jesus into our hearts. Then, as we seek ways to be closer to Him and open our hearts and minds to His presence and how He chooses to reveal Himself to us, we must rest in the knowledge that He is always there with us.

I've been wrestling with how to draw this testimony to a close. Maybe there is no close, because I don't believe that God is anywhere near finished in my life. But, I think I can pause with a poem that He blessed me with several years ago. It seems to wrap up some of the things that I have shared.

# *Strength*

*Somewhere deep inside me,*
*There is a certain place,*
*Where God will sit beside me*
*And fill that empty space.*

*He hears my heart cry out*
*For things I don't understand,*
*And when I'm filled with doubt,*
*He quietly holds my hand.*

*And sometimes when I feel*
*I can go on no more,*
*He shows me that He's real,*
*And opens up a door.*

*He wraps His arms around me,*
*And fills me with His love,*
*And the beauty just astounds me,*
*For it comes from up above.*

*With this comfort I go on*
*Traveling life's winding road,*
*For I know that I can call upon*
*The Lord to share my load.*

# Notes

[1]Martha Whitmore Hickman, *Healing After Loss: Daily Meditations for Working Through Grief* (Avon Books, 1994), p. x.

[2]Max Lucado, *When Christ Comes* (Word Publishing, 1999), pp. 31–62.

[3]Jesse Duplantis, *Heaven: Close Encounters of the God Kind* (Harrison House, 1996), p. 128.

# To Contact the Author:

Email cathygwynn@earthlink.net